Martinis

by James O. Fraioli
with Mixologist Vincenzo Marianella

ALPHA

A member of Penguin Group (USA) Inc.

ALPHA BOOKS

Published by the Penguin Group

Penguin Group (USA) Inc., 375 Hudson Street, New York, New York 10014, USA

Penguin Group (Canada), 90 Eglinton Avenue East, Suite 700, Toronto, Ontario M4P 2Y3, Canada (a division of Pearson Penguin Canada Inc.)

Penguin Books Ltd., 80 Strand, London WC2R 0RL, England

Penguin Ireland, 25 St. Stephen's Green, Dublin 2, Ireland (a division of Penguin Books Ltd.)

Penguin Group (Australia), 250 Camberwell Road, Camberwell, Victoria 3124, Australia (a division of Pearson Australia Group Pty. Ltd.)

Penguin Books India Pvt. Ltd., 11 Community Centre, Panchsheel Park, New Delhi—110 017, India

Penguin Group (NZ), 67 Apollo Drive, Rosedale, North Shore, Auckland 1311, New Zealand (a division of Pearson New Zealand Ltd.)

Penguin Books (South Africa) (Pty.) Ltd., 24 Sturdee Avenue, Rosebank, Johannesburg 2196, South Africa

Penguin Books Ltd., Registered Offices: 80 Strand, London WC2R 0RL, England

International Standard Book Number: 978-1-59257-813-9
Library of Congress Catalog Card Number: 2008924723

10 09 08   8 7 6 5 4 3 2 1

Interpretation of the printing code: The rightmost number of the first series of numbers is the year of the book's printing; the rightmost number of the second series of numbers is the number of the book's printing. For example, a printing code of 08-1 shows that the first printing occurred in 2008.

Printed in the United States of America

Note: This publication contains the opinions and ideas of its authors. It is intended to provide helpful and informative material on the subject matter covered. It is sold with the understanding that the authors and publisher are not engaged in rendering professional services in the book. If the reader requires personal assistance or advice, a competent professional should be consulted.

The authors and publisher specifically disclaim any responsibility for any liability, loss, or risk, personal or otherwise, which is incurred as a consequence, directly or indirectly, of the use and application of any of the contents of this book.

Most Alpha books are available at special quantity discounts for bulk purchases for sales promotions, premiums, fund-raising, or educational use. Special books, or book excerpts, can also be created to fit specific needs.

For details, write: Special Markets, Alpha Books, 375 Hudson Street, New York, NY 10014.

This book is dedicated to all the martini aficionados out there who continue to keep the illustrious cocktail alive.

Contents

Introduction

The martini has been around since the 1800s and remains a fashionable drink today. Due to people's ever-changing tastes, their particular mood that day, the company they're with, or where they happen to be, men and women enjoy a cocktail that satisfies. Unfortunately, one cocktail cannot please everyone, so bartenders created options.

Open any drink menu today, and there's a good chance you'll find the martini. But what you'll also notice is the martinis from the 1950s, '60s, and even the '80s have undergone multiple face-lifts to meet today's demands. In today's martinis, you'll find fresh ingredients, infused liqueurs, and designer touches, while still adhering to the martini's distinctive characteristics of simplicity and sophistication.

In the following pages, you'll find more than 150 delicious martini recipes. In deciding what drinks to feature, professional bartender and mixologist Vincenzo Marianella advised and sampled every martini showcased in this book. Author James O. Fraioli then took these martinis and categorized them into Classic Martinis, Flavorful Fruit Martinis, Aromatic Herb and Vegetable Martinis, Exotic Martinis, Festive Holiday Martinis, and Decadent Dessert Martinis. The result is an updated list of martinis, old and new, that are sure to please—and most importantly, are easy to make at home.

So what are you waiting for? Get a hold of a cocktail shaker, some fresh ice, a few bottles of your favorite spirit, and an assortment of condiments, and begin exploring the magical world of martinis.

Accoutrements

Throughout the book you'll see two kinds of sidebars with garnishes of extra information.

Martini Moment

From historical facts to did-you-know trivia, Martini Moments expand your knowledge of the illustrious cocktail.

Mixology

Not familiar with a particular alcohol or mixer? Don't worry. Mixology sidebars provide bartending insight and educational pointers to help you make the perfect concoction.

Acknowledgments

James would like to thank Mixologist Vincenzo Marianella for his exceptional consultation and martini expertise. Also big thanks to literary agent Andrea Hurst; Kim Busch; Carter Reum and VeeV Spirits; and to my wife, Cindy, who enjoys her vodka martini a bit dirty with three fresh-stuffed blue cheese olives. I alternate between a straight-up gin martini with two olives, and a Manhattan with Woodford Reserve Kentucky Bourbon.

Trademarks

All terms mentioned in this book that are known to be or are suspected of being trademarks or service marks have been appropriately capitalized. Alpha Books and Penguin Group (USA) Inc. cannot attest to the accuracy of this information. Use of a term in this book should not be regarded as affecting the validity of any trademark or service mark.

The Martini

In This Chapter

- Defining the martini
- The ever-evolving martini
- New ingredients, new tastes

From Sir Winston Churchill, Robert Frost, Franklin D. Roosevelt, and William Faulkner, to Humphrey Bogart, Ernest Hemmingway, John F. Kennedy, and Gerald Ford, the martini has been the cocktail of choice for presidents, actors, writers, and even foreign dignitaries, and the tradition continues today.

The martini is as varied as the people who drink it. Some martini drinkers insist on certain ingredients; others swear by entirely different ingredients. Whatever *martini* means to you, you're sure to find a martini recipe (or two, or three, …) you like in the following chapters. But first, let's look at some history of the famous drink.

The Martini Defined

Ask any cocktail connoisseur or purist to define the martini, and he or she will tell you there's only one version that exemplifies the American-born and -bred drink: the classic martini. A chilled glass, a bottle of vodka or gin, perhaps a hint of vermouth, and a lemon twist or an olive, and that's it. Simplicity and sophistication at its finest.

That, my friends, is the definition of the martini.

Martini Moment_____

When Sir Winston Churchill ordered a martini, he would look at a bottle of vermouth from across the room. That's about as close as he would get to adding vermouth to his drink.

But we can't stop there, can we? Variety is the spice of life, after all. You need options. You need to be able to walk into a restaurant or bar and grab that multi-page drink menu to find the perfect drink. Cocktails are meant to be fun, and tastes change depending on the season, mood, company, or even where you're sitting. A classic martini seems a little out of place if you're soaking up the sun on a sugar-white beach in the Bahamas. If you're bundled up in a ski lodge in Aspen, you probably don't want a tropical concoction garnished with a pineapple wedge and a tiny umbrella. Or maybe you do, and because you might, the martini has blossomed into countless varieties of the original.

Whether you crave fruit drinks, sweet drinks, sour drinks, spicy drinks, dessert drinks, or anything in between, it's nice to know you can find a martini perfectly suited to your taste, mood, or setting, no matter where you are. All across America, bars are continuing to experiment with the martini, expanding their drink menus to please, while still serving that classic martini with a smile.

The Birth of the Martini

The town of Martinez, California, claims to be the birthplace of the martini. According to legend there, in 1874, a gold prospector strolled into Julio Richelieu's saloon on Ferry Street, plopped down a sack of gold, and asked the bartender for something other than whisky. When the bartender combined gin, vermouth, and bitters in a glass, the prospector asked what he was making. The bartender replied, "A Martinez."

Martini Moment

The original Martiniz recipe calls for 2 parts gin, 1 part sweet vermouth, and 1 or 2 dashes orange bitters.

Ask folks on the East Coast, and you'll hear a different version of the martini's origins. Just before

World War I, an Italian bartender named Martini di Arma di Taggia from the Knickerbocker Hotel in New York crafted a drink that married gin, dry vermouth, and orange bitters. He named the Martini after himself.

The Brits also claim bragging rights. They argue the heralded drink was named after one of their firearms, the Martini and Henry rifle, because of its enormous kick.

And the stories go on and on, depending on whom you ask.

The Martini Through the Years

In the United States, the martini really took off in the years following Prohibition in the 1920s and early 1930s. By the 1950s, drinking a martini signified you had made it, and consumption of the cocktail became a very glamorous status symbol, similar to driving an expensive sports car or wearing a custom-tailored suit. When James Bond inspired the "vodka martini, shaken not stirred," in the 1960s, the drink was here to stay.

Martini Moment

The James Bond martini first appeared in Ian Fleming's *Casino Royale*. It was also known as the Vesper, named after a beautiful double agent.

By 1980, the martini began to lose its luster and needed a revival. To breathe life into the drink, bartenders began enhancing the martini with fruit juices and catchy names, like the Cosmopolitan. Ten years later, New York's Rainbow Room in Rockerfeller Plaza was famous for its specialty martinis, particularly the "Cosmo." Appletinis, Lemon Drops, and decadent Chocolate Martinis soon followed.

Today, you can find martini bars as part of the libation nightlife in many of the larger cities. These niche bars are known for serving up a bevy of flavorful and intoxicating martini creations, made especially for those craving just that—a martini.

Freshness in Every Glass

Many bartenders and mixologists are replacing concentrates and artificial flavors and sweeteners with real bursts of fruit, vegetables, herbs, and sugars. The colorful bottles of blue Curacao or Midori melon once so lively are falling out of fashion, as are the cocktails that call for them.

Today, manufactured ingredients and artificial mixers are being replaced with natural nectars such as fresh, crisp mint leaves, hand-picked basil, and pure cane sugar. Sweet, luscious blackberries, apples, apricots, cherries, peaches, and strawberries are big hits, too.

Martini Moment

For more fun in your glass, try one of the many vodkas infused with natural fruit flavors such as blueberry, cranberry, orange, pear, pepper, and vanilla.

Drink What *You* Like

The debate of whether to use vodka or gin, or "shaken versus stirred," continues in certain circles, although the martini is constantly being given a modern makeover. Martinis, which once called for only vodka or gin, are now infused with rum, tequila, whisky, and other spirits. Yes, martinis are still shaken and they're still stirred, but now they're also blended, whisked, and whipped.

Regardless of whether you're sipping a sophisticated classic martini or a stylish mojito martini, the most important rule to remember is to drink what *you* like, not what someone else says is the "right" drink.

Whether you prefer to stick to the classics or enjoy sampling the new martinis, one thing is for certain: the martini isn't going anywhere anytime soon.

The Least You Need to Know

- The classic martini consists of vodka or gin, a hint of vermouth, and a lemon twist or olive.

- The debate continues on where the martini originated and who first created the drink.

- Today's martinis are all about fresh ingredients.

- Martinis are classic. They were popular in 1950, they still are today, and they will continue to be in the future.

Tools of the Trade

In This Chapter

- Essential martini-making equipment
- Handy bar tools
- The all-important martini glass
- The finishing touches

You don't need a lot of tools, appliances, or other kitchen gadgets to make great martinis, but you do need some essential tools of the trade. Most are affordable and easy to find, and you probably already have some in your kitchen.

And don't forget the garnish! Whether it's a sprig of fresh mint, an orange twist, or edible flower petals, the right garnish puts the perfect finishing touch on your martini.

Shaken, Not Stirred

All martinis begin with a *cocktail shaker*. These shakers come in a variety of sizes; a medium-size stainless-steel shaker is your best bet. Avoid plastic shakers because they can crack. Also, steer clear of Boston shakers—the 2-cup shaker variety—until you're comfortable behind the bar.

Mixology

The standard **cocktail shaker** is made of three components: a cup, a built-in strainer, and a lid or cap. A vigorous 10- to 15-second shake is all you need to mix and cool the martini in the shaker without the risk of the melting ice diluting the drink.

Cocktail shakers have built-in strainers, but if you're using a tall glass instead of a shaker, you need a strainer to separate the ice from the drink when you pour the martini into the chilled martini glass. I like a professional Hawthorn strainer.

On the Rocks

Martinis are best served cold, and for cold, you need ice. Always use fresh cubed ice, either bagged from the grocery or liquor store or from the trays in your freezer. If you have a block of ice, use a plastic bag, towel, and a hammer or mallet to break it up into more manageable pieces. Add the ice directly to the shaker, before adding any ingredients.

If you haven't previously placed the martini glasses in the freezer to chill before you mix the drink (see the "The Martini Glass" section later in this chapter), you can add the ice directly to the glass to chill it. Just be sure to dump out the ice before you pour in the drink. Martinis are always served *neat*, not *on the rocks*.

Mixology

In bar-speak, **neat** means a drink served without ice. If you want a drink served over ice, ask for it **on the rocks**.

When you're making more than one martini at a time, keep an ice bucket on hand to store the ice until you're ready for it.

Measuring Utensils

As with any other recipe, perfect martinis come from following a recipe, and that means you need to accurately measure your ingredients. Some drink recipes call for ounces, others call for jiggers or shots, and some call for full measures. These are all the same amount, so to make consistent cocktails, get yourself a *bar jigger*.

Mixology

A **bar jigger** is a measure that looks like two cones, joined at the point. One side measures a full measure, or about 1 ounce. The other side measures what's referred to as a *pony*, or ½ ounce.

You probably already have a set of measuring spoons in your kitchen, but if not, get a good set for your bar. They'll come in handy when you need to add sugar or other dry ingredients not measured in the bar jigger.

Bar Tools and Gadgets

If you prefer your martini stirred, not shaken, you need a bar spoon. This long-handled spoon that measures about 1 teaspoon reaches the bottom of the glass or shaker to ensure all ingredients are well combined. If you want to look like a pro when you stir a drink with a bar spoon, twist it with your hands in the same motion you'd use if you were trying to light a fire with a stick.

If a recipe calls for fresh basil or mint, you'll need to mash up the leaves a bit to release their oils and flavor into the drink. For this, you need a *muddler*.

Mixology

A **muddler** is a wooden tool that resembles a miniature baseball bat. Use it to smash or grind herb leaves at the bottom of the glass.

Many martini recipes call for fresh fruit, vegetables, herbs, even seafood, many of which need to be peeled, chopped, or sliced. Always work with sharp, good-quality knives. Use small knives for slicing lemons and limes, and use larger knives for halving melons and large produce.

Along with knives, be sure you have a medium or large cutting board, either plastic or wood. Perhaps get two boards, particularly when you're working with raw seafood, to avoid contamination.

Other tools will be helpful during various martini moments. To be prepared, be sure you have the following:

- Citrus squeezer (to extract fresh lemon or lime juice)
- Corkscrew (handy when non-martini-drinkers arrive with a bottle of wine)
- Graters (good for grating ginger and nutmeg)
- Melon baller
- Vegetable peeler (handy when working with cucumbers)
- Whisk
- Zester (to remove the zest, or top layer, of citrus fruit)

Martini Moment

Citrus squeezers are clean, efficient, and can extract far more juice than your nimble fingers can produce. (And your guests probably prefer not to watch their juice run between your fingers and into their cocktail!) To help loosen the juice inside, roll the fruit several times on a hard surface with the palm of your hand before you cut and juice it.

Small bowls and a pitcher for storing juices are also helpful to have behind the bar.

The only piece of machinery you might need is a blender. A food processor or even that juicer you ordered from a late-night infomercial would also work. For the true bartending aficionado who prefers to make his or her own fruit or vegetable juice from scratch, a blender is a must.

After the martini is shaken or stirred and the garnishes are prepared, it's time to add the final touches. Cocktail sticks are used to hold ingredients like cherries, olives, and cocktail onions together so they don't sink to the bottom of the glass and have to be crudely fished out with the fingers).

Finally, straws. These are not only decorative items that add a splash of color and fun to martinis, but they provide a purpose. It was once customary to drink all cocktails through straws. Today, some folks (women more often than men) like to sip their drink through a straw.

The Martini Glass

Unlike many other cocktails served in bars and homes around the world, the martini is the one drink that requires a particular one kind of glass—the martini glass. The martini glass is elegant, sophisticated, and contains a wide, conical bowl atop a tall, slender stem. Glasses vary in size from 4 fluid ounces to about 10 fluid ounces. Any martini glass larger than 6 or 7 fluid ounces is probably too big.

Martini Moment

Although many varieties and styles of the martini glass have been made, the design remains the same because the large bowl on top keeps the cocktail chilled while the stem keeps the warm hands away.

Before serving a martini, especially to a guest, always inspect the glass. It should be void of chips or cracks, especially along the rim, and the glass should be sparkling clean. Use a glass cloth to remove any dried dishwasher spots.

Martini glasses should also be properly chilled prior to use. The preferred method is to place the glasses in the freezer for about ½ hour, or simply store them in the freezer until ready to use. Another method is to take a room-temperature martini glass, fill it with ice cubes and cold water, and let stand until condensation forms on the inside and outside of the glass. Dump the contents before adding the martini, of course.

Great Garnishes

Keep in mind the "less is more" rule when adding garnishes to martinis. The purpose of a garnish is to accentuate the cocktail, not overpower it. For most martinis, one simple garnish effectively dresses the cocktail, adding color and visual appeal. Some recipes forego the garnish, preferring the à la carte approach.

These are the most common types of martini garnishes:

- Lemon, lime, orange, and grapefruit twists
- Olives
- Fresh fruit
- Fresh vegetables
- Fresh herbs
- Seafood
- Chocolate and other candy

Let's look at how to increase your bartender skills with these garnishes.

Making Citrus Twists

Citrus comes in a variety of shapes and sizes and should reflect the fruit used in the cocktail. Lemons and limes are the most popular fruit behind the bar. Oranges are also common. The *twist* adds elegance to martinis while releasing the fruit's natural oils.

Mixology

A **twist** is a fancy bartending word for a slice of citrus rind—you guessed it—twisted.

To make a citrus twist:

1. Select fresh fruit with bright, clean skin, preferably unblemished.

2. Using a paring knife or vegetable peeler, start at the top of the fruit and peel around the fruit, as if peeling an apple. Work slowly and carefully down the fruit, being sure to keep the rind in one continuous strip.

3. Lay the rind in front of you and, beginning with the edge nearest you, tightly roll the rind to the other end.

4. Keeping the rind tight, use a sharp knife and cut thin, uniform slices across the roll.

5. To finish the twist, take one of the cut slices, twist it over the cocktail, and drop it in the drink.

All About Olives

The olive is the quintessential garnish for many martinis. The most common olive used is the green variety. Select the Spanish Queen olive packed in brine, not oil. Often prestuffed with a pimento, these olives are widely available and ideal for martini lovers, particularly the super colossal size.

If pimento isn't your thing, simply remove the piece of pepper from the olive, or fill the cavity with an ingredient that better compliments the martini you're preparing. Here are some common olive-stuffing ingredients:

- Anchovy
- Blue cheese
- Garlic

- Jalapeño
- Smoked salmon

Creativity is the key because the olive can be stuffed with just about anything that will fit inside the pitted cavity.

Fresh Fruits, Herbs, and Vegetables

Always select fresh, ripened fruits, herbs, and vegetables when garnishing.

Fruits, vegetables, and other small produce items like blackberries, blueberries, cherries, cherry tomatoes, chili peppers, coffee beans, cranberries, and olives are often used whole as a garnish. Herbs like basil and mint are also best when the leaves remain intact.

Large fruits and vegetables, such as apricots, asparagus, strawberries, and jalapeño peppers, are best halved to reduce the size of the garnish.

Larger produce like mango and pineapple are best skinned and sectioned into petite slices or wedges, allowing plenty of room for the drink.

Martini Moment_____

Garnishes like candied gumdrops, chocolate, even cucumber peel should be kept cold to avoid melting or wilting.

Seafood? You Bet!

Not all garnishes are fruits, herbs, and vegetables. Fresh clams and shrimp, or smoked octopus and oysters, make for exotic and interesting garnishes.

When working with seafood, always keep the garnishes on ice or refrigerated.

The Least You Need to Know

- All martinis begin with the bartender's friend—the stainless-steel cocktail shaker.
- A small assortment of bar tools, from citrus squeezers to muddlers to bar spoons, will make your time behind the bar more successful.
- Always pour martinis into pre-chilled martini glasses.
- For the perfect finishing touch, garnishes are a must.

Chapter 3

Classic Martinis

When you're in the mood for something classy and sophisticated, try one of these classic martini recipes. With names that reflect high society, these drinks will be popular at any formal occasion. If you're entertaining guests for a business dinner or hosting a black-tie affair, the Waldorf or the Ivy Club martinis are just two examples of possible cocktails to serve your guests. Impress your co-workers by offering them a Rolls Royce Martini. These are the traditional, standard conceptions of the martini ... with a few added surprises.

Bel-Air Martini

2 oz. *Cointreau*
1 oz. fine cognac
1 oz. fresh lemon juice

Fill a cocktail shaker ½ full with ice. Pour in Cointreau, cognac, and lemon juice. Shake well, and strain into a chilled martini glass.

Mixology

Cointreau is a premium brand of triple sec with a stronger alcohol content.

Belmont Stakes Martini

2 oz. vodka
1 oz. gold rum
½ oz. strawberry liqueur
½ oz. fresh lime juice
1 tsp. grenadine
Lime wedge
Orange slice

Fill a cocktail shaker ½ full with ice. Pour in vodka, gold rum, strawberry liqueur, lime juice, and grenadine. Shake well, and strain into a chilled martini glass. Garnish with lime wedge and orange slice.

Bennett Martini

1½ oz. gin
½ oz. fresh lime juice
2 dashes Angostura *bitters*

Fill a cocktail shaker ½ full with ice. Pour in gin,
lime juice, and Angostura bitters. Shake well,
and strain into a chilled martini glass.

Mixology

Bitters are a concoction of herbs, citrus,
and alcohol, resulting in a bitter taste. Other
ingredients in bitters include Angostura
bark, orange peel, and quinine.

Boston Bullet Martini

2 oz. gin
½ oz. dry vermouth
Almond-stuffed olive

Fill a cocktail shaker ½ full with ice. Pour in gin
and dry vermouth. Shake well, and strain into
a chilled martini glass. Garnish with almond-
stuffed olive.

Bronx Martini

2 oz. gin
1 oz. dry vermouth
1 oz. sweet vermouth
Fresh juice from ½ orange
Fresh cherry

Fill a cocktail shaker ½ full with ice. Pour in gin, dry vermouth, sweet vermouth, and orange juice. Shake well, and strain into a chilled martini glass. Garnish with cherry.

Classic Martini

3½ oz. dry gin
1 tsp. dry vermouth
Lemon twist or olive

Fill a cocktail shaker ½ full with ice. Pour in dry gin and dry vermouth. Shake well, and strain into a chilled martini glass. Garnish with lemon twist or olive.

Martini Moment

When making the Classic Martini, the amount of dry vermouth seems to vary depending on the bartender or the guest. Winston Churchill preferred a full glass of gin with the bottle of vermouth alongside. Alfred Hitchcock enjoyed 5 shots of gin and "a quick glance at a bottle of vermouth."

Detroit Martini

2 oz. vodka
½ oz. *simple syrup*
6 fresh mint leaves
3 dashes orange bitters

Fill a cocktail shaker ½ full with ice. Pour in vodka, simple syrup, and orange bitters. Shake well, and strain into a chilled martini glass. Garnish with mint leaves.

Mixology

Simple syrup is made by combining 1 pound granulated sugar with 1 cup hot water in a saucepan. Simmer until sugar is dissolved, and allow to cool. Pour syrup in a glass bottle, and store in the refrigerator until ready to use.

Diplomat Martini

2 oz. dry vermouth
1 oz. sweet vermouth
Fresh cherry

Fill a cocktail shaker ½ full with ice. Pour in dry vermouth and sweet vermouth. Shake well, and strain into a chilled martini glass. Garnish with cherry.

Dirty Martini

2½ oz. gin
Dash dry vermouth (optional)
1 tsp. olive juice
Olive

Fill a cocktail shaker ½ full with ice. Pour in gin, dry vermouth (if using), and olive juice. Shake well, and strain into a chilled martini glass. Garnish with olive.

Mixology

A **dash** is a bartender's measurement for a small amount of an ingredient, usually about ¹⁄₁₆ teaspoon. It's really up to the bartender to decide how little or how much a dash should be.

Flirtini

1 oz. vodka
¾ oz. Cointreau
2 oz. fresh pineapple juice
Champagne
Fresh cherry

Fill a cocktail shaker ½ full with ice. Pour in vodka, Cointreau, and pineapple juice. Shake well, and strain into a chilled martini glass. Top off with champagne, and garnish with cherry.

Gibson Martini

2½ oz. gin
½ oz. dry vermouth
Cocktail onion

Fill a cocktail shaker ½ full with ice. Pour in gin and dry vermouth. Shake well, and strain into a chilled martini glass. Garnish with cocktail onion.

Green Room Martini

2 oz. dry vermouth
1 oz. brandy
Several dashes Cointreau
Orange twist

Fill a cocktail shaker ½ full with ice. Pour in dry vermouth, brandy, and Cointreau. Stir well, and strain into a chilled martini glass. Garnish with orange twist.

Ivy Club Martini

2 oz. gin
¾ oz. amaretto
¾ oz. fresh lime juice
½ oz. simple syrup
Lime twist

Fill a cocktail shaker ½ full with ice. Pour in gin, amaretto, lime juice, and simple syrup. Shake well, and strain into a chilled martini glass. Garnish with lime twist.

James Bond Martini (a.k.a. Vesper)

3 oz. gin
1 oz. vodka
½ oz. *blond Lillet*
Lemon twist

Fill a cocktail shaker ½ full with ice. Pour in gin, vodka, and blond Lillet. Shake well, and strain into a chilled martini glass. Garnish with lemon twist.

Mixology

Blond (Blanc) Lillet is an aperitif made from Bordeaux wines and liqueurs, with flavors of honey, orange, lime, and mint.

Journalist Martini

3 oz. gin
1 tsp. dry vermouth
1 tsp. sweet vermouth
1 tsp. Cointreau
1 tsp. fresh lime juice
Dash Angostura bitters

Fill a cocktail shaker ½ full with ice. Pour in gin, dry vermouth, sweet vermouth, Cointreau, lime juice, and Angostura bitters. Shake well, and strain into a chilled martini glass.

Loch Lomond Martini

1½ oz. scotch
1 tsp. simple syrup
2 dashes Angostura bitters
Lemon peel

Fill a cocktail shaker ½ full with ice. Pour in scotch, simple syrup, and Angostura bitters. Shake well, and strain into a chilled martini glass. Garnish with lemon peel.

London Martini

3 oz. gin
½ tsp. maraschino liqueur
3 to 5 dashes orange bitters
½ tsp. superfine sugar
Lemon twist

Fill a cocktail shaker ½ full with ice. Pour in gin, maraschino liqueur, orange bitters, and superfine sugar. Shake well, and strain into a chilled martini glass. Garnish with lemon twist.

Manhattan Martini

3 oz. rye whisky or bourbon
1 oz. sweet vermouth
Dash Angostura bitters
Maraschino cherry

Fill a cocktail shaker ½ full with ice. Pour in whisky, sweet vermouth, and Angostura bitters. Shake well, and strain into a chilled martini glass. Garnish with maraschino cherry.

Marilyn Monroe Martini

4 oz. champagne
1 oz. Applejack
1 tsp. grenadine
2 maraschino cherries

In a chilled martini glass, pour in champagne, Applejack, and grenadine. Gently stir, and garnish with maraschino cherries.

Melrose Martini

2½ oz. vodka
¾ oz. Limoncello
½ oz. fresh lime juice
½ oz. simple syrup
¾ oz. fresh cranberry juice
Orange twist

Fill a cocktail shaker ½ full with ice. Pour in vodka, Limoncello, lime juice, simple syrup, and cranberry juice. Shake well, and strain into a chilled martini glass. Garnish with orange twist.

Metropolitan Martini

2 oz. blackcurrant vodka
½ oz. Cointreau
1 oz. fresh cranberry juice
½ oz. fresh lime juice
½ oz. simple syrup
Orange twist

Fill a cocktail shaker ½ full with ice. Pour in blackcurrant vodka, Cointreau, cranberry juice, lime juice, and simple syrup. Shake well, and strain into a chilled martini glass. Garnish with orange twist.

My Fair Lady Martini

1 oz. gin
½ oz. fresh orange juice
½ oz. fresh lemon juice
¼ oz. crème de fraise
1 egg white

Fill a cocktail shaker ½ full with ice. Pour in gin, orange juice, lemon juice, crème de fraise, and egg white. Shake well, and strain into a chilled martini glass.

Opera Martini

3 oz. gin
1 oz. *Dubonnet Blanc*
¼ oz. maraschino liqueur
Lemon twist

Fill a cocktail shaker ½ full with ice. Pour in gin, Dubonnet Blanc, and maraschino liqueur. Shake well, and strain into a chilled martini glass. Garnish with lemon twist.

Mixology

Dubonnet Blanc is a French wine-based aperitif. It's made by adding herbs and botanicals to a fortified white wine.

New York Sour Martini

2 oz. rye whisky
½ oz. freshly squeezed lemon juice
½ oz. simple syrup
¾ oz. pasteurized egg white
½ oz. red wine such as pinot noir
or cabernet sauvignon
Orange twist

Fill a cocktail shaker ½ full with ice. Pour in
whisky, lemon juice, simple syrup, egg white,
and red wine. Shake well, and strain into a
chilled martini glass. Garnish with orange twist.

Park Avenue Martini

3 oz. gin
1 oz. sweet vermouth
1 oz. fresh pineapple juice
Pineapple wedge

Fill a cocktail shaker ½ full with ice. Pour in
gin, sweet vermouth, and pineapple juice. Shake
well, and strain into a chilled martini glass.
Garnish with pineapple wedge.

Poker Martini

1½ oz. white rum
¾ oz. sweet vermouth
2 dashes Angostura bitters
Orange twist

Fill a cocktail shaker ½ full with ice. Pour in white rum, sweet vermouth, and Angostura bitters. Shake well, and strain into a chilled martini glass. Garnish with orange twist.

Reform Martini

2 oz. dry sherry
1 oz. dry vermouth
Dash orange bitters
Maraschino cherry

Fill a cocktail shaker ½ full with ice. Pour in dry sherry, dry vermouth, and orange bitters. Stir well, and strain into a chilled martini glass. Garnish with maraschino cherry.

Rolls Royce Martini

3 oz. gin

1 oz. dry vermouth

1 oz. sweet vermouth

¼ tsp. *Benedictine liquor*

Fill a cocktail shaker ½ full with ice. Pour in gin, dry vermouth, sweet vermouth, and Benedictine liquor. Shake well, and strain into a chilled martini glass.

Mixology

Benedictine liquor is an alcohol made with plants and spices to drink plain, in cocktails, or in culinary preparations.

Russian Martini

2 oz. vodka

2 oz. gin

½ oz. white chocolate liqueur

Fill a cocktail shaker ½ full with ice. Pour in vodka, gin, and white chocolate liqueur. Shake well, and strain into a chilled martini glass.

Taxi Cab Martini (a.k.a. Stone Sour)

2 oz. whisky
¾ oz. fresh orange juice
½ oz. fresh lemon juice
½ oz. simple syrup
2 dashes Angostura bitter
Cherry

Fill a cocktail shaker ½ full with ice. Pour in
whisky, orange juice, lemon juice, simple syrup,
and Angostura bitters. Stir well, and strain into
a chilled martini glass. Garnish with cherry.

Tuxedo Martini

2 oz. vodka
½ oz. dry vermouth
½ tsp. maraschino liqueur
3 to 5 dashes orange bitters
Lemon twist

Fill a cocktail shaker ½ full with ice. Pour in
vodka, dry vermouth, maraschino liqueur, and
orange bitters. Shake well, and strain into a
chilled martini glass. Garnish with lemon twist.

Vanity Fair Martini

3 oz. vodka
1 oz. dark *crème de cacao*
1 oz. half-and-half

Fill a cocktail shaker ½ full with ice. Pour in vodka, dark crème de cacao, and half-and-half. Shake well, and strain into a chilled martini glass.

Mixology

Crème de cacao is a chocolate-flavored liqueur infused with vanilla. The smooth liqueur differs from regular chocolate liqueur due to its sweetness and thickness. In addition to dark crème de cacao, you can find white crème de cacao, a clear form of the same liqueur.

Waldorf Martini

2½ oz. bourbon
¼ oz. *Pernod*
½ oz. sweet vermouth
Dash Angostura bitters
Lemon twist

Fill a cocktail shaker ½ full with ice. Pour in bourbon, Pernod, sweet vermouth, and Angostura bitters. Shake well, and strain into a chilled martini glass. Garnish with lemon twist.

Mixology

Pernod is the brand name of a type of licorice liqueur, produced either with licorice (the plant, not the candy) or anise.

Whisky Martini

3 oz. bourbon
1 oz. Cointreau
2 dashes Angostura bitters
Fresh cherry

Fill a cocktail shaker ½ full with ice. Pour in bourbon, Cointreau, and Angostura bitters. Shake well, and strain into a chilled martini glass. Garnish with cherry.

Flavorful Fruit Martinis

Trying to beat the summer heat? During those long, hot summer days, cool down with a flavorful fruit martini. Although these drinks can be served year-round, they're best in the summer when you can enhance the flavor of the cocktail with the natural sweetness of fresh fruit. Not only does fresh fruit add color and variety to the cocktail, but the fruit's natural sweetness elevates each drink to a higher standard. When purchasing fresh fruit for these delicious martinis, be selective. Always choose fruit that's ripe, has good color, and is free of bruises. For juices, don't buy canned, frozen, or concentrate forms. Purchase only fresh. Or hand-squeeze the juice yourself. It may be more labor intensive, but it's well worth the effort.

Aphrodisiac Martini

1 oz. mandarin vodka

1 oz. citrus vodka

1 oz. Cointreau

½ oz. Chambord

¼ oz. fresh lemon juice

Dash cranberry juice

Dash orange juice

Dash pineapple juice

Dash lemon-lime soda

Fill a cocktail shaker ½ full with ice. Pour in mandarin vodka, citrus vodka, Cointreau, Chambord, lemon juice, cranberry juice, orange juice, pineapple juice, and lemon-lime soda. Shake well, and strain into a chilled martini glass.

Apple Martini

1½ oz. vodka
1 oz. sour apple liqueur
½ oz. Cointreau
½ oz. fresh lime juice
¼ oz. simple syrup
Fresh apple slice

Fill a cocktail shaker ½ full with ice. Pour in vodka, sour apple liqueur, Cointreau, lime juice, and simple syrup. Stir well, and strain into a chilled martini glass. Garnish with fresh apple slice.

Apricot and Mango Martini

1 cup fresh chopped mango, peeled
2 oz. gin
½ oz. apricot brandy liqueur
½ oz. fresh lemon juice
½ oz. simple syrup
Fresh mango slice

In a cocktail shaker, *muddle* chopped mango until well mashed. Fill the shaker ½ full with ice. Pour in gin, apricot brandy liqueur, lemon juice, and simple syrup. Shake well, and strain into a chilled martini glass. Garnish with mango slice.

Mixology

To **muddle** something means to crush it. For example, bartenders use a muddler, a wooden tool that resembles a miniature baseball bat, to smash or grind leaves at the bottom of the glass so oils and flavors of the herbs can be released.

Apricot Martini

2 oz. gin
3 tsp. Dubonnet Blanc
2 tsp. apricot brandy
Dash fresh lemon juice
½ apricot

Fill a cocktail shaker ½ full with ice. Pour in gin, Dubonnet Blanc, apricot brandy, and lemon juice. Shake well, and strain into a chilled martini glass. Garnish with apricot half.

Blackberry Martini

2 oz. blackberry vodka
¾ oz. blackberry liqueur
½ oz. fresh lemon juice
½ oz. simple syrup
Fresh blackberry

Fill a cocktail shaker ½ full with ice. Pour in
blackberry vodka, blackberry liqueur, lemon
juice, and simple syrup. Shake well, and strain
into a chilled martini glass. Garnish with blackberry.

Blueberry Martini

½ cup fresh blueberries
2½ oz. vodka
½ oz. blackberry liqueur
½ oz. fresh lemon juice
½ oz. simple syrup
Fresh blueberries

In a cocktail shaker, muddle blueberries with
vodka until well incorporated. Fill the shaker ½
full with ice. Pour in blackberry liqueur, lemon
juice, and simple syrup. Shake well, and strain
into a chilled martini glass. Garnish with several
blueberries.

Cantaloupe Martini

1 cup fresh cantaloupe, peeled and finely chopped
2 oz. vodka
½ oz. Cointreau
½ oz. fresh lemon juice
½ oz. simple syrup

In a cocktail shaker, muddle cantaloupe until well mashed. Fill the shaker ½ full with ice. Pour in vodka, Cointreau, lemon juice, and simple syrup. Shake well, and strain into a chilled martini glass.

Cherry Martini

½ cup fresh cherries
2 oz. vodka
1 oz. cherry brandy
1 oz. fresh lemon juice
½ oz. simple syrup
Fresh cherry

In a cocktail shaker, muddle cherries with vodka until well incorporated. Add cherry brandy, lemon juice, and simple syrup. Shake well, and strain into a chilled martini glass. Garnish with cherry.

Cloister Martini

2 oz. gin
2 tsp. Yellow Chartreuse
2 tsp. fresh grapefruit juice
1 tsp. fresh lemon juice
1 tsp. simple syrup
Grapefruit twist

Fill a cocktail shaker ½ full with ice. Pour in gin, Yellow Chartreuse, grapefruit juice, lemon juice, and simple syrup. Shake well, and strain into a chilled martini glass. Garnish with grapefruit twist.

Cosmopolitan Martini

2 oz. Citron vodka
½ oz. Cointreau
½ oz. fresh lime juice
Dash simple syrup
½ oz. fresh cranberry juice
Fresh cranberries

Fill a cocktail shaker ½ full with ice. Pour in Citron vodka, Cointreau, lime juice, simple syrup, and cranberry juice. Shake well, and strain into a chilled martini glass. Garnish with several cranberries.

Martini Moment

The origin of the "Cosmo" is somewhat disputed, but most sources credit South Beach, Florida, bartender Cheryl Cook for developing the original creation in the late 1980s.

Florida Orange Martini

1 oz. vodka
1 oz. sweet vermouth
1 oz. fresh Florida orange juice
Dash simple syrup
Orange twist

Fill a cocktail shaker ½ full with ice. Pour in vodka, sweet vermouth, Florida orange juice, and simple syrup. Shake well, and strain into a chilled martini glass. Garnish with orange twist.

French Martini

2 oz. vodka
½ oz. fresh pineapple juice
½ oz. *Chambord*
Lemon twist

Fill a cocktail shaker ½ full with ice. Pour in
vodka, pineapple juice, and Chambord. Shake
well, and strain into a chilled martini glass.
Garnish with lemon twist.

Mixology

Chambord is a raspberry-based liqueur
that includes small black raspberries, red
raspberries, blackberries, currants, herbs,
and spices steeped in cognac and sweetened with honey.

Fresh Fruit Martini

1 cup diced kiwi, strawberry, pineapple, and melon, peeled as necessary
2 oz. vodka
½ oz. simple syrup
½ oz. fresh lemon juice
Dash orange bitters
Fresh kiwi slice

In a cocktail shaker, muddle fruit until well mashed. Fill the shaker ½ full with ice. Pour in vodka, simple syrup, lemon juice, and orange bitters. Shake well, and strain into a chilled martini glass. Garnish with kiwi slice.

Grape Martini

8 fresh seedless red grapes, halved
Dash simple syrup
2 oz. gin
½ oz. fresh lime juice
2 dashes Angostura bitters
3 whole grapes

In a cocktail shaker, muddle halved grapes with simple syrup until well mashed. Fill the shaker ½ full with ice. Pour in gin, lime juice, and Angostura bitters. Shake well, and strain into a chilled martini glass. Garnish with several grapes skewered on a cocktail stick.

Grapefruit Martini

2 oz. vodka
2 oz. fresh grapefruit juice
1 tsp. maraschino liqueur
Grapefruit segment
Maraschino cherry

Fill a cocktail shaker ½ full with ice. Pour in
vodka, grapefruit juice, and maraschino liqueur.
Shake well, and strain into a chilled martini
glass. Garnish with grapefruit segment and
maraschino cherry.

Honeydew Melon Martini

1 cup honeydew melon, peeled and diced
2 oz. vodka
½ oz. Midori melon liqueur
½ oz. fresh lime juice
Dash simple syrup
Fresh mint sprig

In a cocktail shaker, muddle melon with vodka
until well incorporated. Fill the shaker ½ full
with ice. Pour in Midori melon liqueur, lime
juice, and simple syrup. Shake well, and strain
into a chilled martini glass. Garnish with mint
sprig.

Kamikaze Martini

2 oz. vodka
1 oz. Cointreau
1 oz. fresh lime juice
Lime twist

Fill a cocktail shaker ½ full with ice. Pour in vodka, Cointreau, and lime juice. Shake well, and strain into a chilled martini glass. Garnish with lime twist.

Kiwi Martini

1½ oz. gin
2 oz. fresh kiwi juice
¼ oz. fresh lemon juice
½ oz. simple syrup
Fresh kiwi slice

Fill a cocktail shaker ½ full with ice. Pour in gin, kiwi juice, lemon juice, and simple syrup. Shake well, and strain into a chilled martini glass. Garnish with kiwi slice.

Lemon Drop Martini

2 oz. Citron vodka
½ oz. Cointreau
¾ oz. fresh lemon juice
Dash simple syrup
Granulated sugar
Lemon twist

Fill a cocktail shaker ½ full with ice. Pour in
Citron vodka, Cointreau, lemon juice, and simple syrup. Shake well, and strain into a chilled
martini glass rimmed with granulated sugar.
Garnish with lemon twist.

Martini Moment

The Lemon Drop Martini is named after
the popular lemon drop candy, which is
shaped like a miniature lemon.

Lemon Twist Martini

2 oz. light rum
½ oz. fresh lemon juice
½ oz. dry vermouth
Dash simple syrup
Lemon twist

Fill a cocktail shaker ½ full with ice. Pour in
light rum, lemon juice, dry vermouth, and simple syrup. Shake well, and strain into a chilled
martini glass. Garnish with lemon twist.

Lime Martini

2½ oz. vodka
½ oz. Cointreau
¾ oz. fresh lime juice
½ oz. simple syrup
Lime twist

Fill a cocktail shaker ½ full with ice. Pour in
vodka, Cointreau, lime juice, and simple syrup.
Shake well, and strain into a chilled martini
glass. Garnish with lime twist.

Mandarin Orange Martini

2 oz. vodka or Citron vodka
½ oz. mandarin liqueur
½ oz. fresh lemon juice
½ oz. simple syrup
½ oz. fresh orange juice
Orange twist

Fill a cocktail shaker ½ full with ice. Pour in vodka, mandarin liqueur, lemon juice, simple syrup, and orange juice. Shake well, and strain into a chilled martini glass. Garnish with orange twist.

Mango Martini

2 oz. vodka
¾ oz. Mango Passion liqueur
½ oz. fresh lemon juice
¼ oz. simple syrup
1 oz. fresh mango juice
Fresh mango slice

Fill a cocktail shaker ½ full with ice. Pour in vodka, Mango Passion liqueur, lemon juice, simple syrup, and mango juice. Shake well, and strain into a chilled martini glass. Garnish with mango slice.

Orange Blossom Martini

2 oz. gin
½ oz. Cointreau
½ oz. fresh lemon juice
2 oz. fresh orange juice
1 tsp. simple syrup
Edible flower

Fill a cocktail shaker ½ full with ice. Pour in gin, Cointreau, lemon juice, orange juice, and simple syrup. Shake well, and strain into a chilled martini glass. Garnish with edible flower such as a colorful pansy or fragrant rose petals.

Peach Martini

½ fresh peach, peeled and pitted
2 oz. mandarin vodka
½ oz. peach brandy
½ oz. fresh lemon juice
½ oz. simple syrup
2 oz. *Prosecco*
Lemon twist

In a cocktail shaker, muddle peach with vodka until well incorporated. Fill the shaker ½ full with ice. Pour in peach brandy, lemon juice, simple syrup, and Prosecco. Shake well, and strain into a chilled martini glass. Garnish with lemon twist.

Mixology

Prosecco is a sparkling wine made in Italy using the Prosecco grape.

Pineapple Martini

1 cup chopped fresh pineapple
2½ oz. vodka
1 oz. fresh pineapple juice
Pineapple wedge

In a cocktail shaker, muddle chopped pineapple until well mashed. Fill the shaker ½ full with ice. Pour in vodka and pineapple juice. Shake well, and strain into a chilled martini glass. Garnish with pineapple wedge.

Pomegranate Martini

2 oz. vodka

1 oz. fresh pomegranate juice

¾ oz. Cointreau

½ oz. fresh lime juice

½ oz. simple syrup

Lemon twist

Fill a cocktail shaker ½ full with ice. Pour in vodka, pomegranate juice, Cointreau, lime juice, and simple syrup. Shake well, and strain into a chilled martini glass. Garnish with lemon twist.

Purple Haze Martini

2 oz. vodka

½ oz. fresh lime juice

¼ oz. simple syrup

¾ oz. Chambord

Lime twist

Fill a cocktail shaker ½ full with ice. Pour in vodka, lime juice, simple syrup, and Chambord. Shake well, and strain into a chilled martini glass. Garnish with lime twist.

Raspberry Martini

6 to 10 fresh raspberries, 1 or 2 reserved for garnish

2 oz. gin

1 oz. Chambord

½ oz. fresh lemon juice

½ oz. simple syrup

In a cocktail shaker, muddle all but 1 or 2 raspberries with gin until well incorporated. Fill the shaker ½ full with ice. Pour in Chambord, lemon juice, and simple syrup. Shake well, and strain into a chilled martini glass. Garnish with reserved raspberries.

Rum and Fruit Martini

2 oz. light rum

½ oz. fresh orange juice

½ oz. fresh cranberry juice

½ oz. fresh lemon juice

Dash simple syrup

Maraschino cherry

Fill a cocktail shaker ½ full with ice. Pour in light rum, orange juice, cranberry juice, lemon juice, and simple syrup. Shake well, and strain into a chilled martini glass. Garnish with maraschino cherry.

Strawberry and Vinegar Martini

4 fresh strawberries, hulled
4 fresh basil leaves
2 oz. vodka
¾ oz. strawberry liqueur
½ oz. fresh lemon juice
2 dashes simple syrup
¼ oz. aged balsamic vinegar
Fresh strawberry

In a cocktail shaker, muddle strawberries and basil leaves with vodka until well incorporated. Fill the shaker ½ full with ice. Pour in strawberry liqueur, lemon juice, simple syrup, and balsamic vinegar. Shake well, and strain into a chilled martini glass. Garnish with strawberry.

Tangerine Martini

1 oz. vodka
1 oz. sake
1 oz. tangerine juice
¾ oz. Lychee liqueur
Dash simple syrup
3 mint leaves, torn
Fresh tangerine segment

Fill a cocktail shaker ½ full with ice. Pour in vodka, sake, tangerine juice, Lychee liqueur, simple syrup, and mint leaves. Shake well, and strain into a chilled martini glass. Garnish with tangerine.

Walnut Martini

2½ oz. vodka
1 oz. walnut liqueur
1 oz. *Tuaca*

Fill a cocktail shaker ½ full with ice. Pour in vodka, walnut liqueur, and Tuaca. Shake well, and strain into a chilled martini glass.

Mixology

Tuaca is a sweet Italian liqueur golden-brown in color. It's full of brandy, citrus, and vanilla flavors.

Chapter 5

Aromatic Herb and Vegetable Martinis

For those of you who are more health conscious, these herb and vegetable martinis are a unique blend of fresh produce and spices. You won't find your typical Bloody Mary here. For a cocktail with a kick, try a Cajun, Red Onion, or Jalapeño Martini. Or combine your favorite herbs and spices such as basil and thyme with cucumber, rhubarb, or even watermelon. And for a martini that's as traditional as it is simple, savor a Mint Julep Martini. You may also find that some of these recipes, such as the Vanilla Martini, work well as dessert martinis. Find fun ways of mixing health and pleasure with these one-of-a-kind cocktails.

Asparagus Martini

3 oz. vodka

1 oz. blond Lillet

Fresh or pickled asparagus spear

Fill a cocktail shaker ½ full with ice. Pour in vodka and blond Lillet. Shake well, and strain into a chilled martini glass. Garnish with asparagus spear.

Basil and Ginger Martini

3 fresh basil leaves

2 slices fresh ginger root

2 oz. vodka

½ oz. ginger syrup

½ oz. apple liqueur

¾ oz. fresh lemon juice

Fresh basil leaf

In a cocktail shaker, muddle 3 basil leaves and ginger root with vodka. Fill the shaker ½ full with ice. Pour in ginger syrup, apple liqueur, and lemon juice. Shake well, and strain into a chilled martini glass. Garnish with reserved basil leaf.

Martini Moment

To make homemade ginger syrup, add 1 cup water; ½ cup sugar; 5 tablespoons peeled fresh ginger; and 1 vanilla bean, split lengthwise, to a saucepan over medium heat. Cook until sugar dissolves. Simmer for 2 minutes, remove from heat, and let stand 1 hour for flavors to blend. Strain syrup and store in refrigerator.

Basil and Watermelon Martini

1 cup peeled and diced watermelon
6 fresh basil leaves, 1 reserved for garnish
2 oz. gin
½ oz. simple syrup
Fresh lemon juice

In a cocktail shaker, muddle watermelon, all but 1 basil leaf, and gin until well incorporated. Fill the shaker ½ full with ice. Pour in simple syrup and lemon juice. Shake well, and strain into a chilled martini glass. Garnish with remaining fresh basil leaf.

Bloody Mary Martini

1½ oz. vodka
½ oz. fresh lemon juice
1½ oz. tomato juice
1½ oz. beef bouillon
Dash Worcestershire sauce
Dash Tabasco sauce
Salt
Pepper
Sprinkle celery salt
Cocktail onion

Fill a cocktail shaker ½ full with ice. Pour in vodka, lemon juice, tomato juice, beef bouillon, Worcestershire sauce, Tabasco sauce, and celery salt. Shake well, and strain into a chilled martini glass rimmed with salt and pepper. Garnish with cocktail onion.

Martini Moment

In 1934, the St. Regis Hotel in New York added Tabasco sauce to a drink they called the Red Snapper. Not long after, the drink was renamed the Bloody Mary.

Blue Agave Cactus Martini

2½ oz. blue agave tequila
½ oz. *Drambuie*
¾ oz. fresh lime juice
Dash Cointreau
1 tsp. agave nectar
Dash bitters
Orange twist

Fill a cocktail shaker ½ full with ice. Pour in blue agave tequila, Drambuie, lime juice, Cointreau, agave nectar, and bitters. Shake well, and strain into a chilled martini glass. Garnish with orange twist.

Mixology

Drambuie is a golden scotch whisky made with honey, herbs, and spices.

Cajun Martini

2 oz. vodka

1 oz. dry vermouth

2 dashes Tabasco sauce

1 jalapeño pepper

Fill a cocktail shaker ½ full with ice. Pour in vodka, dry vermouth, and Tabasco sauce. Shake well, and strain into a chilled martini glass. Garnish with jalapeño pepper.

Cowboy Martini

2 oz. citrus vodka

½ oz. simple syrup

6 fresh mint leaves

Dash orange bitters

Fill a cocktail shaker ½ full with ice. Pour in citrus vodka, simple syrup, mint leaves, and orange bitters. Shake well, and strain into a chilled martini glass.

Cranberry and Spice Martini

1 oz. dark rum
1 oz. vodka
2 oz. fresh cranberry juice
½ oz. simple syrup
½ oz. fresh lemon juice
Pinch cinnamon

Fill a cocktail shaker ½ full with ice. Pour in dark rum, vodka, cranberry juice, simple syrup, and lemon juice. Shake well, and strain into a chilled martini glass. Sprinkle with cinnamon.

Cucumber Martini

1 cup fresh cucumber, peeled and chopped
2 oz. vodka
½ oz. sake
¼ oz. simple syrup
Strip cucumber peel

In a cocktail shaker, muddle cucumber until well mashed. Fill the shaker ½ full with ice. Pour in vodka, sake, and simple syrup. Shake well, and strain into a chilled martini glass. Garnish with cucumber peel.

English Rosemary Martini

2 sprigs fresh rosemary
2 oz. gin
1 oz. St. Germain
½ oz. simple syrup

In a cocktail shaker, muddle 1 sprig rosemary with gin until well mashed. Fill the shaker ½ full with ice. Pour in St. Germain and simple syrup. Shake well, and strain into a chilled martini glass. Garnish with remaining rosemary sprig.

Garlic Martini

½ clove fresh garlic
3 oz. vodka
1 oz. dry vermouth
Garlic-stuffed olive

In a cocktail shaker, muddle garlic until well mashed. Fill the shaker ½ full with ice. Pour in vodka and dry vermouth. Shake well, and strain into a chilled martini glass. Garnish with garlic-stuffed olive.

Jalapeño Martini

2 thin slices jalapeño pepper
¼ fresh clove garlic
2 oz. vodka
1½ oz. dry vermouth

In a cocktail shaker, muddle 1 slice jalapeño pepper and garlic until well mashed. Fill shaker ½ full with ice. Pour in vodka and dry vermouth. Shake well, and strain into a chilled martini glass. Garnish with remaining jalapeño slice.

Lemongrass and Rhubarb Martini

2 (4-in.) sticks lemongrass
2½ oz. gin
2½ oz. rhubarb juice
2 dashes Angostura bitters

In a cocktail shaker, muddle 1 stick lemongrass with gin until well incorporated. Fill a cocktail shaker ½ full with ice. Pour in rhubarb juice and Angostura bitters. Shake well, and strain into a chilled martini glass. Garnish with remaining lemongrass stick.

Olive and Thyme Martini

Handful fresh thyme
2½ oz. gin
1½ oz. *Green Chartreuse*
½ oz. simple syrup
2 cocktail olives

In a cocktail shaker, muddle thyme with gin until well incorporated. Fill the shaker ½ full with ice. Pour in Green Chartreuse and simple syrup. Shake well, and strain into a chilled martini glass. Garnish with cocktail olives.

Mixology

Green Chartreuse is a natural liqueur made with chlorophyll from more than 130 plants.

Mint and Cranberry Martini

6 fresh mint leaves
2 oz. vodka
1 oz. fresh cranberry juice
½ oz. pomegranate syrup
½ oz. fresh lemon juice
Fresh cranberries

In a cocktail shaker, muddle mint leaves with vodka until well incorporated. Fill the shaker ½ full with ice. Pour in cranberry juice, pomegranate syrup, and lemon juice. Shake well, and strain into a chilled martini glass. Garnish with cranberries.

Mint Julep Martini

10 to 15 fresh mint leaves
1 TB. simple syrup
2 oz. bourbon
Fresh mint sprig

In a cocktail shaker, muddle mint leaves with simple syrup until well incorporated. Fill the shaker ½ full with ice. Pour in bourbon. Shake well, and strain into a chilled martini glass. Garnish with mint sprig.

Martini Moment

The mint julep is the most celebrated cocktail at the Kentucky Derby. During the event, more than 120,000 juleps are served, some fetching as much as $1,000 per julep.

Mojito Martini

5 to 7 fresh mint leaves
2 oz. light rum
½ oz. fresh lime juice
½ oz. superfine sugar
Dash Angostura bitters (optional)
Fresh mint sprig

In a cocktail shaker, muddle mint leaves with rum until well incorporated. Fill the shaker ½ full with ice. Pour in lime juice, superfine sugar, and Angostura bitters (if using). Shake well, and strain into a chilled martini glass. Garnish with mint sprig.

Martini Moment

Mojito is the Spanish name for "mojo sauce," which is also made with fresh lime juice.

Red Onion Martini

3 rings fresh red onion
2 oz. gin
1 oz. sake rice wine
4 dashes orange bitters
½ tsp. simple syrup

In a cocktail shaker, muddle 2 onion rings with gin until well incorporated. Fill the shaker ½ full with ice. Pour in sake rice wine, orange bitters, and simple syrup. Shake well, and strain into a chilled martini glass. Garnish with remaining onion ring.

Sake Martini

1½ oz. gin
2½ oz. sake rice wine
¼ oz. *Grand Marnier*
Lemon twist

Fill a cocktail shaker ½ full with ice. Pour in gin, sake rice wine, and Grand Marnier. Shake well, and strain into a chilled martini glass. Garnish with lemon twist.

Mixology

Grand Marnier is liqueur made from various cognacs along with orange and other ingredients.

Saltecca Martini

2 oz. gold tequila
½ oz. dry sherry
1 tsp. caper juice
Several capers
Lemon twist

Fill a cocktail shaker ½ full with ice. Pour in tequila, dry sherry, and caper juice. Shake well, and strain into a chilled martini glass. Garnish with capers and lemon twist.

Tabasco Martini

2 oz. gin
1 oz. dry vermouth
3 or 4 dashes Tabasco sauce
Green olive

Fill a cocktail shaker ½ full with ice. Pour in gin, dry vermouth, and Tabasco sauce. Shake well, and strain into a chilled martini glass. Garnish with green olive.

Vanilla Martini

3 oz. vanilla vodka
½ oz. Cointreau
½ oz. sweet vermouth
Vanilla bean

Fill a cocktail shaker ½ full with ice. Pour in vodka, Cointreau, and sweet vermouth. Shake well, and strain into a chilled martini glass. Garnish with vanilla bean.

Chapter 6

Exotic Martinis

Perfect for intimate summer evenings or a night in with your loved one, these exotic martinis will leave you feeling beautiful and sexy. Be adventurous with a fruitful Florida Rum Runner Martini or dangerous with a Jolly Roger Martini. Indulge your fantasy of lying on a warm, sandy beach under a bright orange sky by sipping a Caribbean Sunset Martini. With the tropical concoctions in this chapter, you can bring the taste of the islands and faraway places home as you leave your worries behind.

Adonis Martini

2 oz. dry sherry

2 oz. sweet vermouth

2 dashes orange bitters

Orange twist

Fill a cocktail shaker ½ full with ice. Pour in dry sherry, sweet vermouth, and orange bitters. Shake well, and strain into a chilled martini glass. Garnish with orange twist.

Apple Something Martini

2 oz. *Applejack*

1 oz. *St. Germain*

½ oz. fresh lemon juice

¼ oz. simple syrup

¾ oz. organic apple juice

Fill a cocktail shaker ½ full with ice. Pour in Applejack, St. Germain, lemon juice, simple syrup, and apple juice. Shake well, and strain into a chilled martini glass.

Mixology

Applejack is a liqueur made from apples, while **St. Germain** is made with wild elderflowers from the Alps.

Banana Martini

2 oz. vodka
1 oz. crème de banane
½ oz. white crème de cacao
½ oz. light cream
2 drops yellow food coloring
Banana slice

Fill a cocktail shaker ½ full with ice. Pour in
vodka, crème de banane, white crème de cacao,
light cream, and yellow food coloring. Shake
well, and strain into a chilled martini glass.
Garnish with banana slice.

Biscayne Bay Martini

2 oz. gin
1 oz. light rum
1 oz. *forbidden fruit*
1 oz. fresh lime juice
¼ oz. simple syrup
Lime wheel

Fill a cocktail shaker ½ full with ice. Pour in gin,
light rum, forbidden fruit, lime juice, and simple
syrup. Shake well, and strain into a chilled martini glass. Garnish with lime wheel.

Mixology_____

Forbidden fruit is the fruit featured in the
Bible, plucked from the tree of knowledge of good and evil and eaten by
Adam and Eve. In bartending, forbidden
fruits include sliced apple, figs, grapes, or
citrus. Use whatever combination of fruits
you like in your drink.

Caribbean Sunset Martini

2 oz. light rum
½ oz. Cointreau
½ oz. fresh lime juice
¼ oz. simple syrup
Lemon twist

Fill a cocktail shaker ½ full with ice. Pour in
light rum, Cointreau, lime juice, and simple
syrup. Shake well, and strain into a chilled martini glass. Garnish with lemon twist.

Citrus Martini

2 oz. orange vodka
½ oz. Limoncello
½ oz. fresh lemon juice
½ oz. fresh lime juice
½ oz. simple syrup
1 oz. fresh ruby grapefruit juice

Fill a cocktail shaker ½ full with ice. Pour in vodka, Limoncello, lemon juice, lime juice, simple syrup, and grapefruit juice. Shake well, and strain into a chilled martini glass.

Crimson Tide Martini

2 oz. gold rum
¾ oz. apricot brandy
¾ oz. fresh lime juice
½ oz. simple syrup
1 oz. organic guava juice

Fill a cocktail shaker ½ full with ice. Pour in gold rum, apricot brandy, lime juice, simple syrup, and guava juice. Shake well, and strain into a chilled martini glass.

Decadent Elegance Martini

2 oz. cognac
½ oz. *Licor 43*
1 oz. fresh lemon juice
½ oz. vanilla syrup
½ oz. pasteurized egg white
Dash Angostura bitters

Fill a cocktail shaker ½ full with ice. Pour in cognac, Licor 43, lemon juice, vanilla syrup, egg white, and Angostura bitters. Shake well, and strain into a chilled martini glass.

Mixology

Licor 43 is a bright-yellow Spanish liqueur. It's made from citrus and fruit juices and flavored with vanilla and other herbs and spices. **Vanilla syrup** is extracted from vanilla beans and often used to flavor drinks.

Dolores Martini

2 oz. aged rum
1 oz. Dubonnet Rouge
1 oz. dry fino sherry
Dash orange bitters
Lemon twist

Fill a cocktail shaker ½ full with ice. Pour in
aged rum, Dubonnet Rouge, dry fino sherry,
and orange bitters. Shake well, and strain into a
chilled martini glass. Garnish with lemon twist.

Florida Rumrunner Martini

2 oz. white rum
½ oz. blackberry liqueur
1 oz. banana liqueur
1 oz. fresh lime juice
1½ oz. fresh pineapple juice
½ oz. pomegranate syrup
Lime twist

Fill a cocktail shaker ½ full with ice. Pour in
white rum, blackberry liqueur, banana liqueur,
lime juice, pineapple juice, and pomegranate
syrup. Shake well, and strain into a chilled martini glass. Garnish with lime twist.

Flower Martini

3 oz. gin
½ oz. dry vermouth
½ oz. sweet vermouth
Edible flowers

Fill a cocktail shaker ½ full with ice. Pour in gin, dry vermouth, and sweet vermouth. Shake well, and strain into a chilled martini glass. Garnish with edible flower petals.

Martini Moment

Some edible flowers include nasturtiums, marigolds, pansies, and rose petals. If you're not sure if you've picked the correct variety of edible flowers, *do not eat them*. Some flowers are toxic, and some are only edible after appropriate preparations. Do some research to learn to identify and properly prepare flowers for consumption.

Flying Dutchman Martini

2½ oz. soft, full-bodied gin
½ oz. Cointreau
Dash orange bitters
Orange twist

Fill a cocktail shaker ½ full with ice. Pour in gin,
Cointreau, and orange bitters. Shake well, and
strain into a chilled martini glass. Garnish with
orange twist.

Green Dragon Martini

2 oz. vodka
1 oz. Green Chartreuse
Cocktail onion

Fill a cocktail shaker ½ full with ice. Pour in
vodka and Green Chartreuse. Shake well, and
strain into a chilled martini glass. Garnish with
cocktail onion.

Hawaiian Cosmopolitan Martini

2½ oz. vodka
1 oz. fresh pineapple juice
1 oz. fresh apple juice
½ oz. fresh lime juice
¼ oz. simple syrup
Orange twist

Fill a cocktail shaker ½ full with ice. Pour in vodka, pineapple juice, apple juice, lime juice, and simple syrup. Shake well, and strain into a chilled martini glass. Garnish with orange twist.

Hawaiian Martini

2½ oz. gin
½ oz. light fresh orange juice
½ oz. light fresh pineapple juice
½ oz. light fresh lime juice
½ oz. simple syrup
Pineapple slice

Fill a cocktail shaker ½ full with ice. Pour in gin, orange juice, pineapple juice, lime juice, and simple syrup. Shake well, and strain into a chilled martini glass. Garnish with pineapple slice.

Honeysuckle Martini

2 oz. premium aged rum
¼ oz. homemade *honey syrup*
¾ oz. freshly squeezed lemon juice
1 oz. freshly squeezed orange juice

Fill a cocktail shaker ½ full with ice. Pour in aged rum, honey syrup, lemon juice, and orange juice. Shake well, and strain into a chilled martini glass.

Mixology

Honey syrup is a sweetening liquid made by combining 1 cup honey, ¼ cup water, and a dash of cinnamon in a saucepan. Bring to a boil and let simmer for 5 minutes, stirring often. Let cool before using.

Island Martini

2 oz. gold rum
½ oz. dry vermouth
½ oz. sweet vermouth
Lemon twist

Fill a cocktail shaker ½ full with ice. Pour in gold rum, dry vermouth, and sweet vermouth. Shake well, and strain into a chilled martini glass. Garnish with lemon twist.

Jamaican Rose Martini

2 oz. aged rum
¾ oz. amaretto
½ to ¾ oz. freshly squeezed lime juice
½ oz. simple syrup
¾ oz. freshly squeezed grapefruit juice

Fill a cocktail shaker ½ full with ice. Pour in aged rum, amaretto, lime juice, simple syrup, and grapefruit juice. Shake well, and strain into a chilled martini glass.

Jolly Roger Martini

2 oz. light rum
1 oz. Drambuie
1 oz. fresh lime juice
¼ tsp. scotch
½ oz. sparkling water

Fill a cocktail shaker ½ full with ice. Pour in light rum, Drambuie, lime juice, scotch, and sparkling water. Shake well, and strain into a chilled martini glass.

Lyone Martini

2 oz. pear vodka
¾ oz. St. Germain
¼ oz. Green Chartreuse
¼ oz. simple syrup
½ oz. pasteurized egg white
Dash orange bitters
1½ oz. cold ginger beer

Fill a cocktail shaker ½ full with ice. Pour in pear vodka, St. Germain, Green Chartreuse, simple syrup, egg white, and orange bitters. Shake well, and strain into a chilled martini glass. Top with cold ginger beer.

New Orleans Martini

2½ oz. vanilla vodka
1 oz. Pernod
½ oz. dry vermouth
Dash Angostura bitters
Fresh mint sprig

Fill a cocktail shaker ½ full with ice. Pour
in vanilla vodka, Pernod, dry vermouth, and
Angostura bitters. Shake well, and strain into a
chilled martini glass. Garnish with mint sprig.

Poop Deck Martini

2 oz. brandy
1 oz. ruby port
½ oz. blackberry brandy

Fill a cocktail shaker ½ full with ice. Pour in
brandy, ruby port, and blackberry brandy. Shake
well, and strain into a chilled martini glass.

Ramona Martini

2 oz. cane rum

½ oz. apricot brandy

¾ oz. freshly squeezed lemon juice

2 dashes orange bitters

1 tsp. Earth and Vine Papaya Orange
Habanero Preserves

1 jalapeño pepper

Fill a cocktail shaker ½ full with ice. Pour in
cane rum, apricot brandy, lemon juice, orange
bitters, and preserves. Shake well, and strain
into a chilled martini glass. Cut off end of jalapeño and, using your fingers, squeeze out the
juice and oils into the glass. (Be sure to wash
your hands immediately after squeezing jalapeño.) Garnish with a thin slice of pepper.

Ruby Slipper Martini

2 oz. silver tequila
½ oz. *SOHO Lychee* liqueur
½ oz. simple syrup
¾ oz. freshly squeezed lime juice
1 oz. freshly squeezed ruby grapefruit juice

Fill a cocktail shaker ½ full with ice. Pour in silver tequila, SOHO Lychee liqueur, simple syrup, lime juice, and ruby grapefruit juice. Shake well, and strain into a chilled martini glass.

Mixology

SOHO Lychee liqueur is distilled in France using natural Asian lychee fruit. The liqueur is transparent yet sweet.

Rum Martini

3 oz. light rum
½ oz. dry vermouth
Dash orange bitters
Almond-stuffed olive

Fill a cocktail shaker ½ full with ice. Pour in light rum, dry vermouth, and orange bitters. Shake well, and strain into a chilled martini glass. Garnish with almond-stuffed olive.

Sangria Martini

2 oz. dry red wine
¾ oz. cognac
½ oz. apple schnapps
½ oz. Chambord
1 oz. fresh orange juice
½ oz. simple syrup
Orange twist

Fill a cocktail shaker ½ full with ice. Pour in dry red wine, cognac, apple schnapps, Chambord, orange juice, and simple syrup. Shake well, and strain into a chilled martini glass. Garnish with orange twist.

Martini Moment

The blood-red color of the sangria inspired its name, which is Spanish for "bleeding."

Scorpion Martini

1 oz. premium light rum
1 oz. cognac
1½ oz. freshly squeezed orange juice
¾ oz. freshly squeezed lemon juice
½ oz. *almond syrup*

Fill a cocktail shaker ½ full with ice. Pour in light rum, cognac, orange juice, lemon juice, and almond syrup. Shake well, and strain into a chilled martini glass.

Mixology

Almond syrup is a sweetening liquid extracted from almonds often used to flavor drinks.

Shark Attack Martini

3 oz. vodka
1½ oz. fresh lemonade
2 dashes grenadine
Gummy shark

Fill a cocktail shaker ½ full with ice. Pour in vodka, lemonade, and grenadine. Shake well, and strain into a chilled martini glass. Garnish with gummy shark.

Shrimp Martini

3 oz. gin
1 oz. dry vermouth
Dash Tabasco sauce
Cooked shrimp tail, peeled and deveined

Fill a cocktail shaker ½ full with ice. Pour in gin, dry vermouth, and Tabasco sauce. Shake well, and strain into a chilled martini glass. Garnish with shrimp.

Smoked Salmon Martini

3 oz. vodka
½ oz. dry vermouth
Dash fresh lemon juice
Small piece smoked salmon

Fill a cocktail shaker ½ full with ice. Pour in vodka, dry vermouth, and lemon juice. Shake well, and strain into a chilled martini glass. Garnish with smoked salmon.

Summer Breeze Martini

3 oz. vodka

1 oz. Midori melon liqueur

½ oz. pomegranate syrup

¼ tsp. fresh lemon juice

½ oz. cranberry juice

Melon ball

Fill a cocktail shaker ½ full with ice. Pour in vodka, Midori melon liqueur, pomegranate syrup, lemon juice, and cranberry juice. Stir well, and strain into a chilled martini glass. Garnish with melon ball.

Summertime Martini

3 fresh blackberries
3 fresh raspberries
3 fresh strawberries
2 oz. gin
½ oz. fresh lemon juice
½ oz. *crème de mure*
½ oz. Chambord
½ oz. *crème de fraise*
2 dashes orange bitters
Star fruit slice

In a cocktail shaker, muddle blackberries, raspberries, and strawberries with gin until well incorporated. Fill the shaker ½ full with ice. Pour in lemon juice, crème de mure, Chambord, crème de fraise, and orange bitters. Shake well, and strain into a chilled martini glass. Garnish with star fruit slice.

Mixology

Crème de mure is a sweet, blackberry-flavored liqueur. Crème de fraise is a sweet, cream-flavored liqueur often served after dinner.

Sure Thing Martini

1 oz. cane rum
1 oz. bourbon
½ oz. freshly squeezed lemon juice
½ oz. homemade honey syrup
¾ oz. organic pear juice
Pear slice

Fill a cocktail shaker ½ full with ice. Pour in cane rum, bourbon, lemon juice, honey syrup, and pear juice. Shake well, and strain into a chilled martini glass. Garnish with pear slice.

Tahitian Martini

2 oz. white rum
½ oz. fresh lemon juice
½ oz. fresh lime juice
½ oz. fresh pineapple juice
¼ oz. maraschino liqueur
Fresh cherry

Fill a cocktail shaker ½ full with ice. Pour in white rum, lemon juice, lime juice, pineapple juice, and maraschino liqueur. Shake well, and strain into a chilled martini glass. Garnish with cherry.

Tangier Martini

1 oz. gin
1 oz. Cointreau
1 oz. *Mandarine Napoléon* liqueur
Orange twist

Fill a cocktail shaker ½ full with ice. Pour in gin,
Cointreau, and Mandarine Napoléon. Shake
well, and strain into a chilled martini glass.
Garnish with orange twist.

Mixology

Mandarine Napoléon is an orange-
flavored liqueur from Belgium. The key
ingredients are a cognac base, herbal
essence, and the extracted oils from mandarin oranges and tangerine.

Tommy's Margarita Martini

2 oz. 100 percent agave tequila
2 tsp. organic agave nectar
1 oz. fresh lime juice
Lime twist

Fill a cocktail shaker ½ full with ice. Pour in 100
percent agave tequila, agave nectar, and lime
juice. Shake well, and strain into a chilled martini glass. Garnish with lime twist.

Waikiki Martini

3 oz. vodka
1 oz. fresh pineapple juice
½ oz. dry vermouth
½ oz. blond Lillet
Pineapple wedge

Fill a cocktail shaker ½ full with ice. Pour in vodka, pineapple juice, dry vermouth, and blond Lillet. Shake well, and strain into a chilled martini glass. Garnish with pineapple wedge.

Wet Martini

2 oz. gin
1 oz. dry vermouth
Lemon twist

Fill a cocktail shaker ½ full with ice. Pour in gin and dry vermouth. Shake well, and strain into a chilled martini glass. Garnish with lemon twist.

Chapter 7

Festive Holiday Martinis

Get your family and friends in the holiday spirit
with a unique blend of traditional seasonal flavors.
For your next holiday gathering, treat your guests
to one of these fun and festive holiday martinis.
Whether you're serving Shamrock Martinis on St.
Patrick's Day or sipping Eggnog Martinis by the
hearth on Christmas, these unique drinks will bring
out the cheer at any holiday party. Find the mix
that best compliments the theme, and don't forget
to garnish the drink for the occasion. Decorative
holiday glasses are also a nice touch to the perfect
cocktail.

Black Devil Halloween Martini

2 oz. light rum
½ oz. dry vermouth
Black olive

Fill a cocktail shaker ½ full with ice. Pour in
light rum and dry vermouth. Shake well, and
strain into a chilled martini glass. Garnish with
black olive.

Candy Cane Martini

1 oz. vodka
1 oz. Sambuca
1 oz. white crème de menthe
1 oz. white crème de cacao
Miniature candy cane

Fill a cocktail shaker ½ full with ice. Pour in
vodka, Sambuca, white crème de menthe, and
white crème de cacao. Shake well, and strain
into a chilled martini glass. Garnish with miniature candy cane.

Carnival Candied Apple Martini

1 oz. vodka

1 oz. sour apple schnapps

½ oz. amaretto

2 oz. fresh apple juice

Pinch cinnamon

Apple slice

Fill a cocktail shaker ½ full with ice. Pour in vodka, sour apple schnapps, amaretto, apple juice, and cinnamon. Shake well, and strain into a chilled martini glass. Garnish apple slice.

Christmas Martini

3 oz. gin

½ oz. dry vermouth

¼ oz. peppermint schnapps

Mini candy cane

Fill a cocktail shaker ½ full with ice. Pour in gin, dry vermouth, and peppermint schnapps. Shake well, and strain into a chilled martini glass. Garnish with candy cane.

Christmas Snowball Martini

2 oz. gin
1 oz. Pernod
½ oz. half-and-half

Fill a cocktail shaker ½ full with ice. Pour in gin, Pernod, and half-and-half. Shake well, and strain into a chilled martini glass.

Easter Martini

4 green cardamom pods, outer shells removed
2 oz. vanilla vodka
1 oz. white crème de cacao
¼ oz. simple syrup
Chocolate powder

In a cocktail shaker, muddle cardamom pods with vodka until well mashed. Fill the shaker ½ full with ice. Pour in white crème de cacao and simple syrup. Shake well, and strain into a chilled martini glass. Garnish with sprinkle of chocolate powder.

Martini Moment

The green cardamom, the most common cardamom found in high-end grocery stores and markets, is often used as a flavoring for coffee and tea. The spice is best stored in pod form to retain its aromatic fragrance, but ground cardamom can be used in a pinch.

Eggnog Martini

1½ oz. vodka
1 oz. fresh *eggnog*
Dash vanilla extract
Whipped cream
Pinch nutmeg

Fill a cocktail shaker ½ full with ice. Pour in vodka, eggnog, and vanilla extract. Shake well, and strain into a chilled martini glass. Garnish with dollop of whip cream and sprinkle of nutmeg.

Mixology

Eggnog is an American favorite, particularly around Christmas. Find the drink—a blend of milk, cream, sugar, and eggs—fresh or canned.

Elvira Martini

2 oz. gin
½ oz. dry vermouth
1 tsp. Cointreau
2 dashes orange bitters

Fill a cocktail shaker ½ full with ice. Pour in gin, dry vermouth, Cointreau, and orange bitters. Shake well, and strain into a chilled martini glass.

Haunted Bride Martini

2 oz. gin
1 oz. dry vermouth
½ oz. Benedictine liquor
1 tsp. Pernod
2 dashes Angostura bitters

Fill a cocktail shaker ½ full with ice. Pour in gin, dry vermouth, Benedictine liquor, Pernod, and Angostura bitters. Shake well, and strain into a chilled martini glass.

Leap Year Martini

2 oz. gin
½ oz. sweet vermouth
½ oz. Grand Marnier
½ tsp. fresh lemon juice

Fill a cocktail shaker ½ full with ice. Pour in gin, sweet vermouth, Grand Marnier, and fresh lemon juice. Shake well, and strain into a chilled martini glass.

Mardi Gras Martini

2 oz. gin
1½ oz. Dubonnet Rouge
3 to 5 dashes Angostura bitters
3 to 5 dashes Pernod
Maraschino cherry

Fill a cocktail shaker ½ full with ice. Pour in gin, Dubonnet Rouge, Angostura bitters, and Pernod. Shake well, and strain into a chilled martini glass. Garnish with maraschino cherry.

Midnight Black Martini

3 oz. vodka
1 oz. black Sambuca
Black cherry

Fill a cocktail shaker ½ full with ice. Pour in vodka, and black Sambuca. Shake well, and strain into a chilled martini glass. Garnish with black cherry.

Midnight Martini

2 oz. apricot brandy
1 TB. Cointreau
1 TB. fresh lemon juice
Lemon twist

Fill a cocktail shaker ½ full with ice. Pour in apricot brandy, Cointreau, and fresh lemon juice. Shake well, and strain into a chilled martini glass. Garnish with lemon twist.

Mistletoe Martini

2 oz. gin
½ oz. Midori melon liqueur
Dash *grenadine*

Fill a cocktail shaker ½ full with ice. Pour in gin and Midori melon liqueur. Shake well, and strain into a chilled martini glass. Add grenadine.

Mixology

Grenadine is a red syrup, often used in bartending to add color to cocktails. Unlike traditional grenadine made from pomegranates, today, corn syrup and food coloring are the active ingredients.

New Year's Eve Martini

2 oz. light rum
½ oz. Grand Marnier
½ oz. white crème de cacao
½ oz. fresh lemon juice
Dash simple syrup
Lemon twist

Fill a cocktail shaker ½ full with ice. Pour in light rum, Grand Marnier, white crème de cacao, lemon juice, and simple syrup. Shake well, and strain into a chilled martini glass. Garnish with lemon twist.

Nutcracker Martini

2 oz. *crème de noisette*
2 oz. coconut amaretto
2 oz. half-and-half

Fill a cocktail shaker ½ full with ice. Pour in crème de noisette, coconut amaretto, and half-and-half. Shake well, and strain into a chilled martini glass.

Mixology

Crème de noisette is a sweet, chocolate-hazelnut liqueur from France.

Olympic Games Martini

2 oz. brandy
1½ oz. white Curacao
1½ oz. fresh orange juice
Orange twist

Fill a cocktail shaker ½ full with ice. Pour in brandy, white Curacao, and orange juice. Shake well, and strain into a chilled martini glass. Garnish with orange twist.

Peppermint Martini

3 oz. vodka
1 oz. white crème de menthe
Fresh mint sprig

Fill a cocktail shaker ½ full with ice. Pour in vodka and white crème de menthe. Shake well, and strain into a chilled martini glass. Garnish with mint sprig.

Piñata Martini

2 oz. gold tequila
1 oz. crème de banane
1 oz. fresh lime juice
Lime twist

Fill a cocktail shaker ½ full with ice. Pour in gold tequila, crème de banane, and lime juice. Shake well, and strain into a chilled martini glass. Garnish with lime twist.

Presidential Election Martini

2 oz. light rum
½ oz. dry vermouth
½ oz. Cointreau
Dash grenadine
Lemon twist

Fill a cocktail shaker ½ full with ice. Pour in light rum, dry vermouth, Cointreau, and grenadine. Shake well, and strain into a chilled martini glass. Garnish with lemon twist.

Shamrock Martini

2 oz. Irish whiskey
½ oz. dry vermouth
½ oz. green crème de menthe
1 TB. Green Chartreuse

Fill a cocktail shaker ½ full with ice. Pour in Irish whiskey, dry vermouth, green crème de menthe, and Green Chartreuse. Shake well, and strain into a chilled martini glass.

Thanksgiving Martini

1 oz. gin
1 oz. dry vermouth
1 oz. apricot brandy
Dash fresh lemon juice
Lemon twist

Fill a cocktail shaker ½ full with ice. Pour in gin, dry vermouth, apricot brandy, and lemon juice. Shake well, and strain into a chilled martini glass. Garnish with lemon twist.

Witch Martini

1½ oz. vodka
2 oz. tropical fruit juice
½ oz. grenadine
Dash fresh lemon juice
Dash sparkling water
Lemon twist

Fill a cocktail shaker ½ full with ice. Pour in vodka, tropical fruit juice, grenadine, and lemon juice. Shake well, and strain into a chilled martini glass. Top off with sparkling water, and garnish with lemon twist.

Zorro Martini

2 oz. silver tequila
1 oz. plum brandy
1 oz. fresh lime juice
1 tsp. simple syrup
Lime wheel

Fill a cocktail shaker ½ full with ice. Pour in silver tequila, plum brandy, lime juice, and simple syrup. Shake well, and strain into a chilled martini glass. Garnish with lime wheel.

Chapter 8

Decadent Dessert Martinis

When you need to unwind after a long, hard day
with something rich and sweet, try one of these
decadent dessert martinis. If you're craving a fun
and fruity cocktail, try the Apple Pie or Lemon
Meringue Martinis. Perhaps you feel like un-
winding with a warm bubble bath and some
chocolate therapy. In that case, make yourself a
Chocolate Raspberry Martini. For a more romantic
evening for two, serve up a sensual Chocolate-
Dipped-Strawberry Martini. Or bring out your
playful side with a Gumdrop for a Peanut Butter
and Jelly Martini. Take your usual dessert pleasures
and have a little fun with these drinks.

Almond Joy Martini

2 oz. vodka
½ oz. hazelnut liqueur
½ oz. white crème de cacao
Dash fresh coconut milk
Almond

Fill a cocktail shaker ½ full with ice. Pour in vodka, hazelnut liqueur, white crème de cacao, and coconut milk. Shake well, and strain into a chilled martini glass. Garnish with almond.

Martini Moment

Almond Joy is a candy bar made by Hershey's. The sweet treat, created in 1946, is made with coconut and almonds and covered in milk chocolate.

Apple Pie Martini

3 oz. vanilla vodka
½ oz. *Calvados*
½ oz. dry vermouth
Fresh apple slice

Fill a cocktail shaker ½ full with ice. Pour in vanilla vodka, Calvados, and dry vermouth. Shake well, and strain into a chilled martini glass. Garnish with apple slice.

Mixology

Calvados is a potent, apple-based liqueur made from fermented apples in France's Normandy region.

Apple Strudel Martini

½ oz. cinnamon schnapps

1 oz. apple schnapps

1 oz. white crème de cacao

1 oz. fresh apple juice

¾ oz. heavy cream

Pinch cinnamon

Fill a cocktail shaker ½ full with ice. Pour in cinnamon schnapps, apple schnapps, white crème de cacao, and apple juice. Shake well, and strain into a chilled martini glass. Float cream on surface of drink, and garnish with cinnamon.

Banana Cream Pie Martini

2 oz. light rum

½ oz. crème de banane

½ oz. *Godiva white chocolate liqueur*

½ oz. white crème de cacao

¾ oz. heavy cream

Fill a cocktail shaker ½ full with ice. Pour in light rum, crème de banane, white Godiva liqueur, white crème de cacao, and heavy cream. Shake well, and strain into a chilled martini glass.

Mixology

Godiva white chocolate liqueur is a chocolate liqueur produced by Godiva Chocolatier. It's also available in a dark chocolate version.

Banana Split Martini

1 oz. vodka
1 oz. crème de banane
1 oz. Godiva white chocolate liqueur
½ oz. *strawberry syrup*
½ oz. heavy cream
Fresh strawberry

Fill a cocktail shaker ½ full with ice. Pour in vodka, crème de banane, Godiva white chocolate liqueur, strawberry syrup, and heavy cream. Shake well, and strain into a chilled martini glass. Garnish with strawberry.

Mixology

Strawberry syrup is a flavored syrup used to flavor drinks.

Bourbon Cream Float Martini

2 oz. Kentucky bourbon
1 oz. Godiva dark chocolate liqueur
½ oz. heavy cream

Fill a cocktail shaker ½ full with ice. Pour in Kentucky bourbon and Godiva dark chocolate liqueur. Shake well, and strain into a chilled martini glass. Top slowly with heavy cream, creating a top layer of cream only.

Butterscotch Martini

2 oz. vodka
1 oz. butterscotch schnapps
1 oz. white crème de cacao
Butterscotch chips

Fill a cocktail shaker ½ full with ice. Pour in vodka, butterscotch schnapps, and white crème de cacao. Shake well, and strain into a chilled martini glass. Garnish with butterscotch chips.

Café de Paris Martini

2 oz. gin
1 tsp. Pernod
1 tsp. half-and-half
1 egg white

Fill a cocktail shaker ½ full with ice. Pour in gin, Pernod, half-and-half, and egg white. Shake well, and strain into a chilled martini glass.

Cherry Pie Martini

2 oz. vodka
1 oz. brandy
1 oz. cherry brandy
Fresh cherry

Fill a cocktail shaker ½ full with ice. Pour in vodka, brandy, and cherry brandy. Shake well, and strain into a chilled martini glass. Garnish with cherry.

Chocolate-Dipped-Strawberry Martini

4 to 6 fresh strawberries
Melted chocolate
2½ oz. vodka
1½ oz. white crème de cacao

Dip 1 strawberry into melted chocolate and place in the refrigerator to chill. In a cocktail shaker, muddle remaining 3 to 5 strawberries with vodka and white crème de cacao until well incorporated. Fill the shaker ½ full with ice. Shake well, and strain into a chilled martini glass. Garnish with chocolate-dipped strawberry.

Chocolate-Mint Martini

2 oz. light rum
½ oz. white crème de menthe
½ oz. dark Godiva liqueur
Fresh mint sprig

Fill a cocktail shaker ½ full with ice. Pour in rum, crème de menthe, and dark Godiva liqueur. Stir well, and strain into a chilled martini glass. Garnish with mint sprig.

Chocolate-Raspberry Martini

2 oz. raspberry vodka
¾ oz. dark chocolate liqueur
½ oz. simple syrup
¾ oz. half-and-half
Fresh raspberry

Fill a cocktail shaker ½ full with ice. Pour in raspberry vodka, dark chocolate liqueur, simple syrup, and half-and-half. Shake well, and strain into a chilled martini glass. Garnish with raspberry.

Coffee Martini

2 oz. vodka
½ oz. coffee liqueur
1 shot espresso coffee
Roasted coffee beans

Fill a cocktail shaker ½ full with ice. Pour in vodka, coffee liqueur, and espresso coffee. Shake well, and strain into a chilled martini glass. Garnish with roasted coffee beans.

Creamsicle Martini

2 oz. vodka
1 oz. Cointreau
1 oz. fresh orange juice
1 oz. heavy cream
Orange twist

Fill a cocktail shaker ½ full with ice. Pour in vodka, Cointreau, orange juice, and heavy cream. Shake well, and strain into a chilled martini glass. Garnish with orange twist.

Martini Moment

Creamsicle is the brand name for a frozen popsiclelike dessert composed of vanilla ice cream, with an exterior layer of flavored ice, usually orange. American National Creamsicle Day is celebrated every year on August 14.

Honey and Marmalade Martini

2 tsp. honey
2 oz. scotch whisky
1 oz. fresh orange juice
1 oz. fresh lemon juice
Orange twist

In a cocktail shaker, stir honey and scotch whisky until well incorporated. Fill the shaker ½ full with ice. Pour in orange juice and lemon juice. Shake well, and strain into a chilled martini glass. Garnish with orange twist.

Gumdrop Martini

2 oz. rum
¾ oz. fresh lemon juice
½ oz. Southern Comfort
Dash dry vermouth
Lemon twist
Gumdrops

Fill a cocktail shaker ½ full with ice. Pour in rum, lemon juice, Southern Comfort, and dry vermouth. Shake well, and strain into a chilled martini glass. Garnish with lemon twist and several gumdrops.

Jelly Belly Martini

1½ oz. white rum
1 oz. peach schnapps
1 oz. coconut rum
2 dash orange bitters
Jelly Belly jelly beans

Fill a cocktail shaker ½ full with ice. Pour in white rum, peach schnapps, coconut rum, and orange bitters. Shake well, and strain into a chilled martini glass. Garnish with several Jelly Belly jelly beans.

Key Lime Pie Martini

2 oz. vodka
1 oz. Midori melon liqueur
1 oz. fresh lime juice
1 oz. heavy cream
Dash Angostura bitters
Graham cracker crumbs
Lime twist

Fill a cocktail shaker ½ full with ice. Pour in vodka, Midori melon liqueur, lime juice, heavy cream, and Angostura bitters. Shake well, and strain into a chilled martini glass rimmed with graham cracker crumbs. Garnish with lime twist.

Lemon Meringue Martini

2 oz. light rum
½ oz. *Limoncello*
½ oz. Cointreau
½ oz. fresh lemon juice
Lemon twist

Fill a cocktail shaker ½ full with ice. Pour in light rum, Limoncello, Cointreau, and lemon juice. Shake well, and strain into a chilled martini glass. Garnish with lemon twist.

Mixology

Limoncello is an Italian liqueur made with lemon peels, clear grain alcohol, water, and sugar. It's sweet, lemony, and best served chilled.

Lollypop Martini

1 oz. Green Chartreuse
1 oz. *kirshwasser*
1 oz. Cointreau
1 tsp. maraschino liqueur

Fill a cocktail shaker ½ full with ice. Pour in Green Chartreuse, kirshwasser, Cointreau, and maraschino liqueur. Shake well, and strain into a chilled martini glass.

Mixology

Kirschwasser is a clear cherry brandy made in Germany. It's sometimes called simply *kirsch*.

Macaroon Martini

3 oz. vodka
½ oz. Godiva white chocolate liqueur
½ oz. amaretto
Orange twist

Fill a cocktail shaker ½ full with ice. Pour in vodka, Godiva white chocolate liqueur, and amaretto. Shake well, and strain into a chilled martini glass. Garnish with orange twist.

Maple and Peanut Butter Martini

½ tsp. creamy peanut butter
½ tsp. honey
2½ oz. vodka
1 oz. maple syrup
½ oz. crème de banane

In a cocktail shaker, stir peanut butter and honey with vodka until well combined. Fill the shaker ½ full with ice. Pour in maple syrup and crème de banane. Shake well, and strain into a chilled martini glass.

Mudslide Martini

1 oz. vodka
1 oz. Baileys Irish Cream
1 oz. dark crème de cacao

In a cocktail shaker, add vodka and Baileys Irish Cream. Add ice, and stir to chill. Strain into a chilled martini glass. Drizzle dark crème de cacao on top.

Orange Delight Martini

2 oz. orange vodka
1 oz. Cointreau
1 oz. fresh orange juice
2 orange twists
½ tsp. confectioners' sugar

Fill a cocktail shaker ½ full with ice. Pour in orange vodka, Cointreau, and orange juice. Stir well, and strain into a chilled martini glass that's been moistened on the rim with 1 orange twist and dipped into confectioners' sugar. Garnish with remaining orange twist.

Peanut Butter and Jelly Martini

5 to 7 fresh raspberries
1½ oz. vodka
1 oz. Frangelico hazelnut liqueur
2 oz. fresh cranberry juice

In a cocktail shaker, muddle 3 to 5 raspberries with vodka until well combined. Fill the shaker ½ full with ice. Pour in Frangelico and cranberry juice. Shake well, and strain into a chilled martini glass. Garnish with remaining raspberries.

Martini Moment

A recent survey showed that the average American will have eaten 1,500 peanut butter and jelly sandwiches before graduating from high school.

Southern Cream Pie Martini

2½ oz. Kentucky bourbon
1 tsp. superfine sugar
½ oz. light cream
Nutmeg

Fill a cocktail shaker ½ full with ice. Pour in Kentucky bourbon, sugar, and light cream. Shake well, and strain into a chilled martini glass. Garnish with sprinkle of nutmeg.

Swiss Alps Chocolate Martini

1 oz. vodka

1 oz. Godiva white chocolate liqueur

1 oz. white crème de cacao

1 oz. light cream

Chocolate shavings

Fill a cocktail shaker ½ full with ice. Pour in vodka, Godiva white chocolate liqueur, crème de cacao, and light cream. Shake well, and strain into a chilled martini glass. Garnish with sprinkle of chocolate shavings.

Tootsie Roll Martini

3 oz. vodka

½ oz. Godiva dark chocolate liqueur

½ oz. Grand Marnier

Orange twist

Fill a cocktail shaker ½ full with ice. Pour in vodka, Godiva dark chocolate liqueur, and Grand Marnier. Shake well, and strain into a chilled martini glass. Garnish with orange twist.

Tutti Frutti Martini

1 oz. orange vodka

1 oz. raspberry vodka

1 oz. Chambord

1 oz. fresh orange juice

1 oz. cranberry juice

Lime twist

Fill a cocktail shaker ½ full with ice. Pour in orange vodka, raspberry vodka, Chambord, orange juice, and cranberry juice. Shake well, and strain into a chilled martini glass. Garnish with lime twist.

White Licorice Martini

2 oz. vodka

1 oz. white crème de cacao

½ oz. Sambuca

½ oz. light cream

Fill a cocktail shaker ½ full with ice. Pour in vodka, white crème de cacao, Sambuca, and light cream. Shake well, and strain into a chilled martini glass.

Glossary

almond syrup   A sweetening liquid extracted from almonds often used to flavor drinks.

Applejack   A liqueur made from apples.

bar jigger   A measure that looks like two cones, joined at the point. One side measures a full measure, or about 1 ounce. The other side measures what's referred to as a *pony*, or ½ ounce.

Benedictine liquor   An alcohol made with plants and spices to drink plain, in cocktails, or in culinary preparations.

bitters   A concoction of herbs, citrus, and alcohol, resulting in a bitter taste. Other ingredients include Angostura bark, orange peel, and quinine.

Blond (Blanc) Lillet   An aperitif made from Bordeaux wines and liqueurs, with flavors of honey, orange, lime, and mint.

Calvados   A potent, apple-based liqueur made from fermented apples in France's Normandy region.

Chambord   A raspberry-based liqueur that includes small black raspberries, red raspberries, blackberries, currants, herbs, and spices steeped in cognac and sweetened with honey.

cocktail shaker   A bartending tool comprised of a cup, a built-in strainer, and a lid or cap. A vigorous 10- to 15-second shake is all you need to mix and cool a martini without risk of the melting ice diluting the drink.

Cointreau   A premium brand of triple sec with a stronger alcohol content.

crème de cacao   A chocolate-flavored liqueur infused with vanilla. The smooth liqueur differs from regular chocolate liqueur due to its sweetness and thickness. In addition to dark crème de cacao, you can find white crème de cacao, a clear form of the same liqueur.

crème de fraise   A sweet, cream-flavored liqueur often served after dinner.

crème de mure   A sweet, blackberry-flavored liqueur.

crème de noisette   A sweet, chocolate-hazelnut liqueur from France.

dash   A bartender's measurement for a small amount of an ingredient, usually about $\frac{1}{16}$ teaspoon. It's really up to the bartender to decide how little or how much a dash should be.

Drambuie   A golden scotch whisky made with honey, herbs, and spices.

Dubonnet Blanc   A French wine-based aperitif. It's made by adding herbs and botanicals to a fortified white wine.

eggnog   An American favorite, particularly around Christmas. Find the drink—a blend of milk, cream, sugar, and eggs—fresh or canned.

forbidden fruit   The fruit featured in the Bible, plucked from the tree of knowledge of good and evil and eaten by Adam and Eve. In bartending, forbidden fruits include sliced apple, figs, grapes, or citrus.

Fraise   A strawberry liqueur, used to add flavor and sweeten certain cocktails.

full measure   A measure equivalent to about 1 ounce.

Godiva liqueur   A chocolate liqueur produced by Godiva Chocolatier. It's available in white chocolate and dark chocolate versions.

Grand Marnier   Liqueur made from various cognacs along with orange and other ingredients.

Green Chartreuse   A natural liqueur made with chlorophyll from more than 130 plants.

Grenadine   A red syrup, often used in bartending to add color to cocktails. Unlike traditional grenadine made from pomegranates, today, corn syrup and food coloring are the active ingredients.

honey syrup   A sweetening liquid made by combining 1 cup honey, ¼ cup water, and a dash of cinnamon in a saucepan. Bring to a boil and let simmer for 5 minutes, stirring often. Let cool before using.

Kirschwasser A clear cherry brandy made in Germany.

Licor 43 A bright-yellow Spanish liqueur. It's made from citrus and fruit juices and flavored with vanilla and other herbs and spices.

Limoncello An Italian liqueur made with lemon peels, clear grain alcohol, water, and sugar. It's sweet, lemony, and best served chilled.

Mandarine Napoléon An orange-flavored liqueur from Belgium. The key ingredients are a cognac base, herbal essence, and the extracted oils from mandarin oranges and tangerine.

muddler A wooden tool that resembles a min-iature baseball bat. Use it to smash or grind the leaves at the bottom of the glass so oils and flavors of the herbs can be released.

neat A drink served without ice.

on the rocks A drink served over ice.

Pernod A type of licorice liqueur, produced either with licorice (the plant, not the candy) or anise.

pony A measure equivalent to about ½ ounce.

Prosecco A sparkling wine made in Italy using the Prosecco grape.

shot A measure equivalent to about 1 ounce.

simple syrup A sweetening liquid made by combining 1 pound granulated sugar with 1 cup hot water in a saucepan. Simmer until sugar is dis-solved, and allow to cool. Pour syrup in a glass bot-tle, and store in the refrigerator until ready to use.

SOHO Lychee liqueur   A transparent yet sweet liqueur distilled in France using natural Asian lychee fruit.

St. Germain   A liqueur made with wild elderflowers from the Alps.

strawberry syrup   A flavored syrup used to flavor drinks.

Tuaca   A sweet Italian liqueur golden brown in color. It's full of brandy, citrus, and vanilla flavors.

twist   A fancy bartending word for a slice of citrus rind—you guessed it—twisted.

vanilla syrup   A sweetening liquid extracted from vanilla beans often used to flavor drinks.

Index of Drinks

A

B

C

D

E-F

G

H-I

N–O

P–Q

R

S

T–U–V

W–X–Y–Z